I would like to acknowledge the traditional owners of the land where these words have been written.

I would like to acknowledge the Woi-Wurrung and Boon-Wurrung people of the Kulin Nation. Also acknowledging the Nuoenonne people of the island state of the Lutruwita, where I grew up and have spent a lot of my life.

I would like to pay my respects to all First nations people that have come before us and that will come after us. I want to thank the Traditional Custodians for caring for this Country for generations.

It is important understand that to this day, the land in which I and others conduct themselves is land that was stolen from all Indigenous people and that sovereignty was never ceded.

This continent always was and always will be Aboriginal land.

SKY DADDY

Copyright © 2022 by UserNameUnknown

All rights reserved. No part of this book may be reproduced in any manner whatsoever without written permission except in the case of brief quotations embodied in critical articles and reviews.

First Printing, 2022

USERNAMEUNKNOWN

SKY DADDY

UserNameUnknown

CONTENTS

Dedication
i

I Am Tired of Poetry
1

Fact or Fiction?
3

Spectrum Questioning
5

Priceless Silence
7

Dear Heavenly Father
9

Leopard
11

Grim Reaper
12

Gibberish
14

EP Content
15

Carrots Come to Life
16

Not a Poem
18

Humans and Rodents
20

Terra Australis
22

Soliloquy
24

CONTENTS

About The Author
28

I AM TIRED OF POETRY

I am tired of my poetry
I am tired of the words I have written

I am tired of going over each letter with a magnifying glass, attempting to find more meaning, all to justify the time spent on writing them

I am tired of re-reading everything over and over again
I am tired of ink filled notebooks that continue to say nothing

I am
A nervous poet, sitting in the corner of the room, anxiety coursing through their veins
Wondering:
"What the fuck am I doing here?"
Racing thoughts, convinced their truth is not enough truth to be true
The crowd feeling like a pack of wild hyenas waiting to pick apart another corpse, striping what flesh is left from the bone

I am
A woman deciding to pull out that short, low cut red dress at the back of the wardrobe, convinced that it was never suited for any occasion
Throwing self-doubt to the wind, simply to go out for a couple of drinks with friends on a Tuesday night because fuck it, I know my cleavage and legs will make jaws drop
Turning heads that want what they deserve to never have

I am
A boy sitting in class, confused after being told he was not to spend time around girls during school
Teachers paranoid of a potential satanic death orgie manifesting itself, creating a black hole of debauchery that no letter from the principal in the weekly newsletter could ever explain

Encouraged instead to spend time with the same sex but at the same time quoting from the bible about how homosexuality is a sin against god
So to honour him, he's taught through the good word that if he is to be respectful, he is not to watch porn for 'chances are' he will grow up to rape and murder, upsetting jesus

He is a good little christian now
He can go forth and marry a nice girl, despite the unhealthy ideology about women that had been perpetuated during his most important years of growing up

With all questions answered with 'jesus'

Teachers knew best and teenagers were cruel

I am
That one kid who came here as a refugee, attending the same school, where no one looks or speaks like me but nonetheless at their mercy, hoping they accept me for me
All I see are nervous smiles and hearing the silence of neglecting voices

Teachers knew best and teenagers were cruel

I am
No longer a cruel teenager, my eyes now see a different world
They see a world through borrowed lenses but sadly, with glasses I wish I never broke
Glasses I cannot fix
But still try to anyway

I am

You

And you are poetry

FACT OR FICTION?

Who is it today?

Whose sirens song will my ship be wrecked upon?

Dr Jekyll?
Mr Hyde?

On one hand:
Sociable, respected, put together, but it all feels fake to me

The other:
Remorseless, hidden, aggressive, but the source of creativity

Most days, it feels as if the doctor is being torn apart limb from limb, and even when he tries to run, there is never anywhere to, Hyde

A losing battle
Nothing more than an execution
Slowly poisoning myself with my linguistic elocution
No serum that I take, no pill that I ingest makes this duality any clearer

Perhaps I am already the very evil I thought I never could be?
A Frankenstein's monster, a misunderstood experiment, stitched together from pieces of other people's perceived reality

Choosing to accept fantasy written on pages of fiction, blindly discriminating without restriction
Plagued by a collective fear
Lighting torches, sharpening pitchforks, protecting themselves from an evil they know only through tales told by others
It's simply easier to remove those things we wish not to understand

Exhausted from trying to make people understand, exhausted from clinging to the hope that strangers feel safe about their own lives

While I stay vigilant
Waiting for the day that the same angry mob finally comes for me

USERNAMEUNKNOWN

So, who is it today?

Whose sirens song *will* my ship be wrecked upon?

Dr Jekyll?
Mr Hyde?
Is it Frankenstein's monster?

Will I have to wait until someone else writes a character in which I can finally be compared to?
A character that requires no torches, no pitchfork
No unprecedented fear

I may always be a misunderstood experiment
I refuse to be the fictional reality on someone else's page

People are tired of reading
No space left upon their bookshelf
Dust covered volumes of wasted stories

SPECTRUM QUESTIONING

"You know, a lot of experts think being on the spectrum's not a disorder. Some think it might even be the next evolutionary step."
- The Predator, 2018

I have questions:

Is the justification for the exploitation of environmental problem solving warranted for involuntary evolution manipulation?

Or is it about perception?

If not mirroring the T.V.
Does it get the same reception?

Or white noise static?
Is a brain useful if lacking the wrong type of sellable mental magic?
What exactly should occur compared to where the profit is?

I suppose the answer lies in the pockets of executives
Having a grotesque focus on a marketable diagnosis
Pandering to the common denominator of the lowest

What needs replicating and which characteristics does one need to portray to become a sellable autistic?
How can one rationalise concepts from the past
While claiming we're futuristic?

Despite a reality they do not live in
Profiting off others mental health for a living

It's disability appropriation
Taking away self determination
Disagree and never recognise
Feel free to trivialise
And see whatever you want with your own eyes
Nit picking some rendition
To create a condition, emphasising rating recognition

Suffice to say
I ain't much defined by the criticism
Living in a realm of precision, my own prism of a selfish ambition

So enjoy your inspiration porn fetishism
Journey through emotional tourism and arriving at your contrived optimism
Where narratives negate negative critique, deemed as sensationalism

While life drains from the strangulation of one's agency
Blinded by the entertainment value to see your own complacency

Although I'm not here to compare resilience
Too many already with selfish ambivalence
Claiming some kind of false equivalence
I'm just trying to test the limits of my own existence

PRICELESS SILENCE

I want my words to mean something
I want to provide something of substance

I do not want to speak for anyone else
Experiences deserve to be told by those who own them
But infinite stories inevitably go untold

Eagerly silenced by authority
Silenced by privilege
Silenced by doctrines
Silenced by a duty to believe
Silenced by beliefs never consented to
Silenced by those they trusted

With no trumpet to blow
Stuck behind the fortified walls of Jericho
Forced to walk back into the lion's den
Again, and again and again

Wondering why they are the only one who can see the gnashing teeth and sharp claws
The irony being no one would believe in something they cannot see themselves

Every passage read from scriptures becomes words ignored from written confessions inside a diary
of a child who is too scared to speak
Every arm filled with the cuts of a razor creates unheard symphonies drowned out by a cacophony
of prayers and hymns

A congregation placated for shameless commodification
Becoming arbiters of their own creation
With closed ears, deaf to their righteous indignation

Please still donate and tithe
To a business built on lies
A heaven-sent ten percent
Open those pearly gates
While still dressed in a cloak and holding a scythe

Forked tongued politicians
A story too familiar
The same old renditions
Of a worthless Prime Minister

Readjust what's discussed with unjust cover ups
It corrupts the trust but it's a must to keep that crust

Dollars lining pockets of legislation
Status quo regulation
Cash flow verses through divine manipulation

Money talks
It's incessant

But silence

Silence is priceless

DEAR HEAVENLY FATHER

Dear heavenly father,

I think this will be the last time I ever dedicate a poem about you

Because those three words,
They do not feel the same anymore
Since you decided to close that window and forgot to open that door

Although I still remember talking to you every night hoping I would be granted comfort while I tossed and turned
But despite all my hopeful thoughts and all my devoted prayers, *you* heavenly father taught me that I didn't need to be asleep to have nightmares

My restless insomnia was at the behest of a false guardian angel I believed was looking down, protecting me

It turned out to be nothing but mere fabrication of my own naïve, wishful imagination
You created a brain that was perfectly designed for manipulation

Blindly allowing it to be controllable
A piece of clay easily mouldable
Shaped by another's hand
Forgoing my own existence, to do your biding, at your will and command

I saw the world through rose tinted glasses
My vision has changed as time passes
I now see that wickedness was woven within worshipping words as you watched as I withered away without concerns

Your narcissistic insecure omnipotence showed me that, to you, I was of no importance

One thing I will do, I'll confess to *my* sinfulness and how it's become limitless and although blasphemous, *my* ubiquitous wickedness has caused,

A mess

They say it's lonely at the top

Then why did I find myself alone on the ground floor, hearing only whispers from ghosts that refuse to leave me in peace?

I've burnt all my spiritual bridges and you are to blame
I've had to stand there, looking back at those apparitions through heathenish flame

Valuable lessons have been learned though
You taught me that heaven is where true evil chose to lurk
And that you are not holy, you're doing the devils work

Scriptures say that I am wrong and that you are merciful
Therefore, please forgive me father for I have sinned
I believed in false idols
Before I believed in myself

LEOPARD

They say a leopard cannot change its spots

That evolution has created for it a linear trajectory towards a path predetermined by forces outside its control
Forced to accept its role within nature, bound by a hierarchy that has given it an apparent predetermined existence outside the realms of controllability

Those spots become the admiration of everyone
All those eyes and yet still blind to what those spots truly mean to the Leopard

Unable to be proud, those spots have become nothing more than camouflage to hide itself away
Evolving to merely adapt to its surroundings, not out of any desire, for survival

Self-preservation becomes the number one priority
For it knows it can fall victim to a poacher taking predatory aim down the scope of their rifle
A silencer fitted to their barrel, suppressing any possibility of detection, affording them the ability to reload and fire again if they miss their target

It only takes one bullet
One to become a trophy on someone else's wall, another casualty added to a secretive body count that no one wants to acknowledge out of fear

A dichotomy that manipulates the process of evolution to benefit the predatory actions of a collective group that benefits off that fear it creates

Attempting to diminish what it takes to ignite the catalyst to form a creature from what it is, to what it will be, to what it deserves be

Petrified of allowing it to evolve into a powerful creature and not constrained by the actions of those who mean to do it harm

They cannot allow those spots to evolve to become bullet proof, for an unkillable creature does not fear becoming a trophy anymore

GRIM REAPER

I wrote a poem the other week
Committing the ultimate cardinal sin:

Convincing myself I'd remember what to write down and say
The best laid plans of mice and men mean nothing if paper never meets the pen

All I do remember:

I was sitting alone in the park, lost in my own mind
As the sun shone down, for a brief moment I wasn't lost in thought because

Nothing mattered

Simply living in that exact point in time, there was peace and quiet
Cynicism stripped momentarily from my brain and all that I heard was the sound of magpies
replacing any thought that tried to deafen me

Contentment
The only word to describe it

But like all good things, they come to an end
As regrettably reality reappears
Continuing to unavoidably occur

Getting distracted by fractures in practice

What I witnessed was a man standing there releasing birds into the sky
Until a big enough flock formed and began circling above his head

All the birds strangely seemed to have both wings that were right
All they can do is keep circling, unable to turn left when in flight

The image was interrupted by the echoing sound of a gun being fired
I jumped for cover hoping not to get hit, when I peeked my head out from behind a tree
I saw that same man aiming a rifle into the air, taking pot shots at those same birds he just released

SKY DADDY

Plumes of feathers exploding
Gently raining down to the ground

The man looked lifeless, as though he was neither enjoying what he was doing
Nor showing any distain for his actions

I watched until this man took every last bird from the sky, leaving nothing but silence and destruction

He turned to me, his eyes were empty and before too long a shadowy figure appeared behind him, dressed in a cloak, scythe in hand, the smell of corruption stung my nostrils
Within an instant the man disappeared, the gun fell to the floor to join the creatures it had destroyed

I walked home, whatever contentment I had felt now long dissipated, trying to make sense of what I witnessed unfold before my eyes

I lay staring at my ceiling that night, wide awake pondering the vivid images that poured inside my mind

I wrote a poem the other week

I wrote it down, nothing this time made me forget to put pen to paper
Sadly, it does not capture any whimsical moment

All I could remember to write was:

That the grim reaper does not fear death
It does not worry about who takes their final last breath
It does not fear any weapon or any bullet
It does not care about the trigger or who happens to pull it
It takes no responsibility for the destruction it reaps from
Souls are collateral, just as long as we succumb

I just want to go back and sit in the park
Or better yet
Live within utopian ecstasy and simply forget

GIBBERISH

Empty pages of a notebook lay dormant on the table
A pen sits beside it, ready to write the words locked away inside a mind that does not know how to form them into anything other than incoherent gibberish
Days lost through tormenting alphabetical waves of thought, desperately trying to piece together a linguistic puzzle that scatters itself amongst the already cluttered mind that hurriedly searchers for the remaining hidden pieces
Forced into daydreaming, for night seems to only ever grant a reality where sleep becomes a distant memory where a naïve past that held such comforting ignorance, cocooned away from what now keeps you awake
A hallucinogenic state of consciousness replaces an existence plagued by meanderings of idol hypocrisy initiated by zealous and intrigued onlookers that ultimately fail to keep your attention
Disturbed by trivial endeavours that only serve to placate you in scenarios that deserve no recognition from an uncompromising fortitude, but, nonetheless exists with provocative malice
Contemplating sadistic imagery as more than mere soulless reassurance which mimics any sense of perception which eases one's troubled existence
Compelled by translucent voices heard not by another's ear, a manifestation of such false pretences, masking the true maleficent agenda of the self but ultimately taking a contrived solace in that it is something still of your own making
That a safe haven of thoughts may not always culminate inside, these thoughts nonetheless indicate you are still alive
Fortuitous encounters formulate daily rituals that curtail promising strides towards betterment, but opportunity overrides the ability to acknowledge dangerous patterns that distract from the pursuit of a societal wholesomeness
Exhausted from systematic doctrines moulded into a narrative with such evil comforts you fight against those thoughts succumbing to a harmonious morality, unknowingly indoctrinated to fulfil the needs of those who choose to destroy a sacred bond of those who wish to live amongst each other's with no more than passing thoughts of contentment.
Preserving a legacy that withstands no test of time

EP CONTENT

This part of the book are the lyrics from the Sky Daddy EP as the title suggests

CARROTS COME TO LIFE

There are days where I feel as though my brain does not deserve my existence
Battling a fight of cognitive dissonance
A confusing reality imprisoning us
Corrupting innocence
The ambivalence of calculated brilliance

Still navigating what is it to be alive
Still navigating how best to live, exist and how to thrive
Rhyming words are fine
Although they don't pay the rent or these bills of mine

Nothing I write is perfect and I want to be perfect
My pursuit of perfectionism personified plainly by personality
This perfect person persona is a ridiculous, unattainable endeavour
A concept that consistently haunts me forever

So, what's to blame to for this warped ideology?
Maybe it's the ADHD and my inability to think rationally or possibly the ASD and the retard trying to burst from the chest cavity
Paradoxically, he don't wear his heart on his sleeve
Making poignancy nigh on impossible to to achieve

Try as I might
They
Just
Wont
Fucking
Leave

We all have to fight some kinds of demons
Rolling dice with the devil just to see who wins
Its a complexity that perplexes me with letters that seemingly define my poetry

I'm still searching for another definition
I'm still waiting for the correct premonition

Embarking on this soulless endeavour of validation that's honestly not worth the tireless linguistic creation
For this relentless ambitionlessness is at the behest of every witness

Becoming a faceless performative Sisyphus
Because my god, I'm getting bored of all this

NOT A POEM

I'm nothing but the Horrific atrocity
Stargazer Ptolemy Capricorn astrology
Unknown horror of the scope of blasphemy
The unholiest G.O.A.T

The antithesis of what could never be hypothesised
So imagine with your eyes their rigorous hypothesis

A story teller with those caldron tales
Toiling the trouble bubbling the details
Pickpocketing surface level never fails
Forming opinions like they're dragon scales

Bootleg divergence from shadowy merchants
With wrongful insurgence of neuro-occurrence
Flogging products for social insurance
Don't have to be Jedi to feel that disturbance

Lightsabre swinging for the fences
Relentless assault on the core senses

Rhythmic psychiatrist
Demons fought, fingers balled, fist violence
The purist form of the quietist alliance
Herculean laborious compliance
Got my hands tied its a duct tape escape
Hook line sinker fishing boat bait
Counting down served on a plate
To a pack of hyenas as they salivate

Embalmed in the blatant mummification
Wrapped up in ancient gratification
Lost to rising tides of selfish diatribes
Waves crashing with clouds to coincide
With lightening that hits twice in the same storm
A coffee drinker tea cup, hive mind honey swarm

SKY DADDY

It's guaranteed come hell or highwater
X marks the spot, a modern-day marauder

Stolen pen tricks the abysmal abyss the building blocks made from straw and sticks
Sketching blueprints with the fabled bricks architect copywritten penmanship linguistics

The huffing and the puffing rhyme talker
The Big Bad Wolf, Little Pig stalker
White coat stethoscope wrong diagnosing
Teeth exposed and fast approaching

The one existing
Syringing content to find what's worth binging

Lost patience to waiting room games
Setting aflame concepts never to reclaim
Perilous maze, treacherous challenges
Turning corners in the labyrinth of imbalances
In the absence of talentless badges to warrant the malice in someone else's palace

Without a Hitchcock trying to save face
A Psycho with that switch and bait
Errorless stumbling in a Minotaur chase
Drinking from a chalice in a Daedalus race

A self fulling prophecy
Outsourced created but with no apology

Drinking from a chalice in a Daedalus race

HUMANS AND RODENTS

Let me explain, every chapter like a Dictionary
Cant understand? Then I'll sketch it like its Pictionary

Scribbled solutions masquerading as delusions
It's all there fused in some written down conclusions

I got these sceptics tripping on the rhetoric
Can't accept the hallucinogenic ink trick

Gripping thought amateurs sipping saboteurs absentee connoisseurs
Opinion whisperers

I'm quick to think and I'm slow to talk x4

No ascension to paradise but then again
The best laid plans of any mice and men
Showing us omnipotence aint never been heaven sent
Homemade Kool-Aid for entertainment

An enormous amorphous Morpheus
Lullabies sung for us, a flawless chorus
Mistaking that dream state for something worth it weight
Grandiose delusions now becoming our true fate

Relevant precedent sits dormant as sentiment
Staying sediment self-evident intelligence
Perceived as decadence through a venomous malevolence
Forming a tumultuous hippocampus with eloquence

I'm quick to think and I'm slow to talk x4

No ascension to paradise but then again
The best laid plans of any mice and men
Showing us omnipotence aint never been heaven sent
Homemade Kool-Aid for entertainment

Rhyming becoming the cure the new Ritalin

SKY DADDY

Helping slow the head space I'm always stuck in
Still hearing slurred words occur, so lets begin
Taking aim at all the wolves covered in sheepskin

A majestic jester sitting in the royal courts
Listening to kings and queens as they talk
About
Wars they've started but haven't fought
Eyes never caught the sight of a lifeless corpse

No ascension to paradise but then again
The best laid plans of any mice and men
Showing us omnipotence aint never been heaven sent
Homemade Kool-Aid for entertainment

TERRA AUSTRALIS

The scariest variant of any proletariat
Cut throat cut string crazy marionette
I'm Boudica on her chariot, causing panic
Crashing front lines of bourgeoisie demographic

Fighting those who have everything lose
Throwing friends to the wolves when they're asked to choose
No alliance, no neutrality
The enemy of my enemy is still an enemy to me

Turncoats with swords to the throats
Action determined through back pocket banknotes

In joyful strains then let us sing
A sorrowful chorus of suffering

See no evil, hear no evil, then speak none
Blind eyes lips shut then its job done
Information coming from the barrel of the gun
Suppressed written bullets, it only takes one
x2

The cataclysmic Kalashnikov
Bullets spraying, damnation now becoming the pay off
I defy any neophytes
Freezing hell over losing fingers through the frostbite
Fingerless acolytes trying to get a slice
Hard to hold a knife if you've paid the price

My madness a descending ascendancy
So the higher powers stopped believing in me

I'll still be dinning with the gods on Mount Olympus
Or dancing with hades where the river Styx is
Death means nothing to the grim reaper
I'll be quiet when I'm a permanent dirt sleeper

SKY DADDY

I'll haunt you like the corpse bride
Zombified, don't dead, open inside

In history's page, let every stage
Forget chapters of horrific rearrange

See no evil, hear no evil, then speak none
Blind eyes lips shut then its job done
Information coming from the barrel of the gun
Suppressed written on bullets, it only takes one
x2

In joyful strains then let us sing
A sorrowful chorus of suffering
In history's page, let every stage
Forget chapters of horrific rearrange

SOLILOQUY

Sycophantic romantics trying to finesse financial
chances with hollow antics
Freely keeping secrets like a Mason
Staying stone faced brazen with commandment breaking

Deceptive sculptures, incestuous objectives
Ineffective Medusa collectives
Vultures with tumultuous narrative
False additives, tortuous preservative

It's all food for thought but I'm still hungry
I want some tucker for my rumbling tummy
This kaleidoscopic vision imprisons ambition
Submission of cognition has now risen

Forced to manifest with the rest, told more is less
Forget what you feel inside your chest
Becoming too dark for stars to glisten
Only a supernova under supervision

Its whether or not we can weather the weather
Drowning ourselves under all this pressure
Walking in the rain only makes you wetter
Grab an umbrella, we can go together

Spare a dollar? Running out of cents
I'm making even less
Sparing no expense
Creating significance of nothing
Clinging to false brilliance and then pretending that it's something

The diligence of corruption we aren't from
The pricelessness we all miss out on
Battling serpentine temptation
Eat the apple, forbidden manipulation

SKY DADDY

Coerced but never reimbursed
Trying to float to the top before your bubbles burst
It's joke, like who's on first
Home runs only for the well versed

Walking that tight rope lyricism
Balancing our optimism
Dodging the precision of contrived altruism
Idolising false realism
Work hard and play harder
Gram fiends online fire starter
Light dreams but fall even harder
Spit you out then discard ya

Its whether or not we can weather the weather
Drowning ourselves under all this pressure
Walking in the rain only makes you wetter
Grab an umbrella, we can go together

Self restrictions, the noose tightens
Losing consciousness as the tunnel brightens
The only way to meet my maker
Is the mirror reflecting the created perpetrator

The source of me is sorcery
Unknown forces and flights of fantasy
Keep experimenting, the right catalyst
To make gold, linguistic alchemist

And if its not magic
The fabric of each breath becomes problematic
Each syllable of a soliloquy
Is a pentamic mindset mutiny

Its whether or not we can weather the weather
Drowning ourselves under all this pressure
Walking in the rain only makes you wetter
Grab an umbrella, we can go together

Given an synthetic anaesthetic
From authentic prophetic heretics
Providing us with irrelevant aesthetic
Saying what you what to do the tricks

Holding control but it's getting looser
The fogs too thick to claim to see the future

Trying to figure our what your life's worth
The price you've paid since you've been given your birth

The downfall from the crystal ball
Comforting words now becoming subliminal

That's it
I've said it all
I've said it all

CONCLUSION

FIN

This book is a passion project, it was not able to happen without the assistance of Arts Access Victoria and the Victorian Government. I was accepted to receive a grant to help disabled artists with a project they would like to achieve. This project included the writing and printing of this book as well as writing, recording and the release of an EP.

UserNameUnknown lives in Victoria, Australia. He hasn't studied and form of poetry, literature or other types of writing, he just started to write poems and over time developed and improved his style and skills. Performing his work has provided him the ability to understand and navigate the poetry scene which has helped form the way he writes his and performs his pieces.
He MCs a poetry night and has always been a strong advocate for the advancements of promoting and allowing new poets to speak, perform and feel connected to a community. Joining up with a local music collective, Vibe Union, he has dived into the world of rap and has begun to write and perform his own songs.

There isn't much more to say about this author at this very moment, they may write another book at some point but for now they hope you enjoy this one.

Cover art designed by @Rhath_Music & @VibeUnion

www.ingramcontent.com/pod-product-compliance
Lightning Source LLC
Chambersburg PA
CBHW060534010526
44107CB00059B/2641